50 Learning Songs
Sung to Your Favorite Tunes

Teach & Delight Every Child With Skill-Building Songs
That Are Fun to Sing & a Snap to Learn!

by Meish Goldish

SCHOLASTIC
PROFESSIONAL BOOKS

New York • Toronto • London • Auckland • Sydney
Mexico City • New Delhi • Hong Kong • Buenos Aires

Dedication

To my daughter Sarah,
my favorite singer

Cover design by Kelli Thompson

Cover artwork by Jane Conteh-Morgan

Interior design by Sydney Wright (based on a design by Solutions by Design, Inc.)

Interior artwork by Sue Dennen

ISBN: 0-439-24878-7

Table of Contents

Introduction 4

Reading and Writing

Letters and Names 7

Vowels 8

Consonants 10

Period 11

Question Mark 12

Exclamation Point 13

Rhyming Words 14

Read a Book 16

Be an Author! 17

Primary Concepts

Opposites 18

Left and Right 19

Days of the Week 20

Months of the Year 21

Four Seasons 22

Mathematics

Telling Time 23

Money 24

Adding 25

Take Away 26

Skip Counting 28

Patterns 29

Pairs 30

Fractions 31

Weigh and Measure 32

Social Studies

Library 33

School 34

The Market 36

At the Fire Station 37

The United States 38

The President 39

Our Flag 40

Hello Around the World 41

December Holidays 42

The Pilgrims 43

Social Skills

Say "Please" 44

Say "Thank You" 45

Solving Problems 46

Sharing 47

Taking Turns 48

Listening 49

Friendship 50

Science

Animal Sounds 51

Animal Groups 52

Eggs 53

Life of a Frog 54

Bugs 55

Dressing for Weather 56

Five Senses 57

My Body 58

Trees 60

Planting a Garden 62

Sun and Moon 63

Book Links 64

Introduction

What's the way most children learn the letters that later will become words they read and write? By singing their way through the alphabet song! The alphabet song is a perfect example of the magic of music and its power to motivate learning and make it stick. This book features 50 learning songs sung to familiar tunes that you can use to strengthen skills and concepts in every corner of your curriculum. The following are activities you can use to teach with these songs and extend the learning.

Picture Book Songs

Your students can turn the songs they learn into sing-along picture books. Invite students to copy each line of a song (or verse) on a separate sheet of paper, then illustrate it. Arrange the pages in order and bind to make a book. (Be sure students include a cover and the name of the tune the song is sung to.)

Sing-Along Surprise

Build music into your day with a "sing-along surprise." Write each child's name on a slip of paper and place it in a bag or box. Explain that each day (or every Friday, for example) you'll select a child's name. This child will get to choose any moment of the day for the class to sing a song! Provide a bell (or some other way) for the student to signal that it's time for the sing-along. Stop what you're doing and enjoy a learning song together!

Name That Tune!

Invite groups of children to take turns humming a learning song. Can the class name that tune? For example, if a group hums the tune of "Row, Row, Row Your Boat," students would correctly guess "Read a Book," the learning song sung to this tune.

Sight-Word Game Boards

Turn any of the songs into a "game board" for building reading and writing skills. Here are three quick games to play:

- ᗌ Sight-Word Reading Relay: After listening to or singing a song, write it on chart paper and gather students around. Say a sight word and give one child a pad of sticky notes. Have that child cover up that word and pass the sticky notes to another child. Say another sight word and let that child cover it up. Continue until you've covered all of the target words.

- ᗌ Word Riddles: Say, "I'm thinking of a word between [insert the two words in the song that your mystery word falls in between]." Invite a child to find your word, then make up the next riddle.

- ᗌ Word Detectives: Reinforce just about any phonics skill with a word-finding game. Say you're singing the song "Days of the Week." (See page 20.) You might start by asking children if they can find 11 words with a long /a/ sound. Next, you might point out the word *like* and challenge them to find another word in the song with the same /i/ sound. Continue, using any phonics focus to lead the way. Offer plenty of praise along the way for your young detectives' sharp eyes and strong skills!

Morning Meeting Songs

As you introduce new songs to children, copy them on a chart paper pad. Each day, invite a different child to choose a song for the class to sing. Make a sparkly wand for children to use to point out the words as the class sings the song. For more fun, let children decide whether they want to sing the song soft or loud, slow or fast.

> **Tip**
>
> To make a wand, glue a star cut from sturdy paper to a dowel or ruler. Dab on glitter glue and tie on curly ribbon.

Shake, Rattle, and Sing

Make simple instruments that students can use to reproduce the rhythm of songs they sing. Here are some quick-and-easy instruments to make:

- ᗌ Give each child a bathroom tissue tube. Have children cover the tubes with paper and decorate them. Cut circles from paper that are about an inch bigger than the openings of the tubes. Have children cover one opening with paper and use tape to secure it. Give each child some dried beans or unpopped corn to

place in the tube. Have children cover the other end securely and shake! For more fun, tape streamers or curly ribbons to both ends of the tube.

~ Tap old spoons together to play the "castanets."

~ Turn empty, clean yogurt containers (with the lids on) into drums. Use the eraser-end of pencils as drumsticks.

~ Cut up a sheet of corrugated cardboard into pieces that are about 8" x 10" each. Tape a cardboard "handle" to the smooth side. Have children slip their hands through the handle, then play this instrument by scraping the corrugated side with an unsharpened pencil or a ruler.

Record Your Singing Stars

Children will have fun recording the songs they learn. Each time students learn a new song, record it on an audio tape. Place the tape and cassette recorder at a listening center, along with copies of the songs. (You may want to laminate them and place them in a binder.) Let children listen independently as they follow along on the song sheets.

Pocket Chart Play

Many of the songs in this book have lines that end in rhyming words. Write the words to these songs on sentence strips. Cut apart the rhyming words. Place the sentence strips and word cards in a pocket chart. As you sing the song, let children replace the missing words in the song, using the spelling patterns as clues. Do more with word families by inviting children to suggest other words that rhyme. Write these words on sentence strips and trim to size. Group rhyming words and look at the spelling together. Do the same letters make the same sounds?

Letters and Names

(sung to "The Alphabet Song")

ABCs are so much fun,
Spelling names for everyone!
Every letter starts a name,
Now let's play a little game:
Naming names from A to Z,
See what you can spell with me!

A is Amy, B is Brett,
C is Carlos and Collette,
D is Donna, E is Ed,
F is Frankie, Fran, or Fred,
G is Ginger, H is Hal,
I is Ike and Isabel.

J is Janet, K is Kyle,
L is Lewis, Lee, or Lyle,
M is Mary, N is Ned,
O is Oscar and Odette,
P is Peter, Q is Quinn,
R is Roy and Rosalynn.

S is Suki, T is Thad,
U is Ursa, V is Vlad,
W is Will or Wong,
X is Xavier, Y Yvonne,
Z is Zoe, that's our game,
Every letter starts a name!

Vowels

(sung to "Old MacDonald Had a Farm")

CHORUS:

Which five letters are the vowels?
A-E-I-O-U.
Which five letters are the vowels?
A-E-I-O-U.

With an A, A here, and an A, A there,
Here an A, there an A, everywhere an A, A.
Which five letters are the vowels?
A-E-I-O-U.

CHORUS

With an E, E here, and an E, E there,
Here an E, there an E, everywhere an E, E.
Which five letters are the vowels?
A-E-I-O-U.

CHORUS

With an I, I here, and an I, I there,
Here an I, there an I, everywhere an I, I.
Which five letters are the vowels?
A-E-I-O-U.

CHORUS

With an O, O here, and an O, O there,
Here an O, there an O, everywhere an O, O.
Which five letters are the vowels?
A-E-I-O-U.

CHORUS

With a U, U here, and a U, U there,
Here a U, there a U, everywhere a U, U.
Which five letters are the vowels?
A-E-I-O-U.

CHORUS

Consonants

(sung to "Oh, Dear, What Can the Matter Be?")

CHORUS:

Tell me, what are the consonants?
Tell me, what are the consonants?
Tell me, what are the consonants?
Which letters do they include?

B, C, and D, these letters are consonants,
F, G, and H, these letters are consonants,
J, K, and L, these letters are consonants,
M is a consonant, too.

CHORUS

N, P, and Q, these letters are consonants,
R, S, T, V, these letters are consonants,
W, X, Y, these letters are consonants,
Z is a consonant, too.

CHORUS

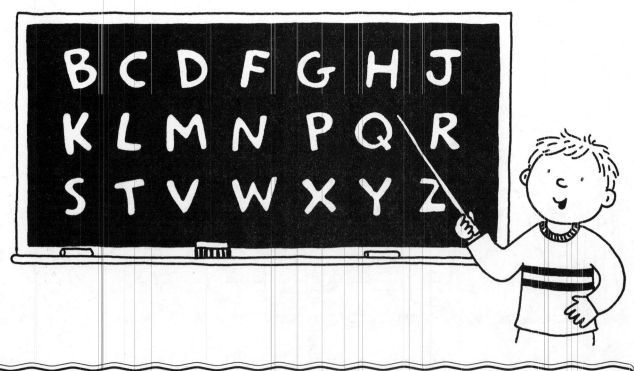

50 Learning Songs Scholastic Professional Books

Period

(sung to "I'm a Little Teapot")

I'm a little period,
Small and round.
After a statement,
I'll be found.
If there's information,
I am there.
At the very end,
That's where.

I'm a little period,
One round dot.
I'm very small,
But used a lot.
If you make requests,
Then I'll be there.
Look and find me.
Be aware.

Question Mark

(sung to "Where, Oh Where, Has My Little Dog Gone?")

CHORUS:

Oh where, oh where does a question mark go?
Oh where, oh where should it be?
Is it at the end of a question, my friend?
Why don't you look here and see?

Do you have something that you'd like to ask?
What is your question, my friend?
When you write a question, do you always add
A question mark at the end?

CHORUS

What time is it? What's for dinner tonight?
Will you please be my best friend?
When you read a question, do you always find
A question mark at the end?

CHORUS

Can you find question marks here in this song?
Where do you see them, my friend?
When you see a question, do you always find
A question mark at the end?

CHORUS

Exclamation Point

(sung to "Bingo")

I know a punctuation mark,
It's used to show emotion!

CHORUS:

Exclamation point!
Exclamation point!
Exclamation point!
It's used to show emotion!

Oh, golly gee! Well, look at me!
Oh, wow! That's some emotion!

CHORUS

Oh, me! Oh, my! How pleased am I!
Oh, gosh! That's some emotion!

CHORUS

Ka-boom! Ka-pow! Such noise, and how!
Oh, dear! That's some emotion!

CHORUS

Look out! Beware! Hey, that's not fair!
Oh, yes! That's some emotion!

Rhyming Words

(sung to "Do You Know the Muffin Man?")

CHORUS:

Do you know the words that rhyme,
The words that rhyme, the words that rhyme?
Do you know the words that rhyme?
Their endings sound the same!

Do you know what rhymes with me?
Bee and tea and he and we,
Three and see and free and tree,
Their endings sound the same!

CHORUS

Do you know what rhymes with bed?
Bread and fed and red and sled,
Said and led and sped and head,
Their endings sound the same!

CHORUS

bee

tea

bed

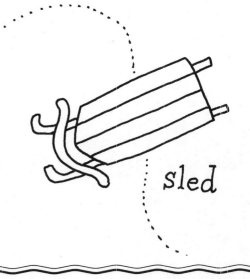

sled

50 Learning Songs Scholastic Professional Books

Do you know what rhymes with you?
True and blue and two and shoe,
Do and new and boo-hoo-hoo!
Their endings sound the same!

CHORUS

Do you know what rhymes with I?
Try and by and tie and why,
Cry and fly and high and sky,
Their endings sound the same!

CHORUS

Do you know what rhymes with go?
Slow and know and show and toe,
Blow and grow and ho-ho-ho,
Their endings sound the same!

CHORUS

shoe

boo
hoo
hoo

fly

go!

grow

tie

Read a Book

(sung to "Row, Row, Row Your Boat")

Read, read, read a book,
Read a book today!
Learn about, learn about, learn about, learn about
Places far away!

Read, read, read a book,
Read a book to know!
Know about, know about, know about, know about
People long ago!

Read, read, read a book,
Read it with a friend!
Page by page by page by page,
Until you reach the end!

Read, read, read a book,
Read a book for fun!
Fantasy, mystery, comedy, history,
Books for everyone!

Read, read, read a book,
Read a book tonight!
Pick a book, pick a book, pick a book, pick a book,
Read—it's such delight!

Be an Author

(sung to "Found a Peanut")

CHORUS:

Be an author, be an author,
Be an author, day or night!
It's so fun to be an author,
There is so much you can write!

Write a story, an adventure,
With explorers or with spies!
Be an author, write a story,
Give it mystery and surprise!

Write a poem for your best friend,
Write of fall or summertime.
Be an author, write a poem,
Give it rhythm, make it rhyme.

Write a joke or write a riddle,
Tell about a blue giraffe!
Be an author, write a riddle,
Make it funny, make 'em laugh!

Write a letter to your cousin,
Tell about the things you do.
Be an author, write a letter,
Say what's happening, tell what's new.

CHORUS

Opposites

(sung to "Ten Little Indians")

You say yes, and I say no,
You say stop, and I say go,
You say fast, and I say slow,
These are opposites!

You say day, and I say night,
You say dark, and I say bright,
You say heavy, I say light,
These are opposites!

You say big, and I say small,
You say short, and I say tall,
You say none, and I say all,
These are opposites!

You say wet, and I say dry,
You say low, and I say high,
You say laugh, and I say cry,
These are opposites!

You say hot, and I say cold,
You say bought, and I say sold,
You say young, and I say old,
These are opposites!

You say fat, and I say thin,
You say lose, and I say win,
You say out, and I say in,
These are opposites!

Left and Right

(sung to "Hokey Pokey")

I'm pointing to my left,
I'm pointing to my right,
I'm pointing to my left,
And it makes me very bright!
You see, I know directions
To the left and to the right.
That makes me very bright!

I'm looking to my left,
I'm looking to my right,
I'm looking to my left,
And it makes me very bright!
You see, I know directions
To the left and to the right.
That makes me very bright!

I'm stepping to my left,
I'm stepping to my right,
I'm stepping to my left,
And it makes me very bright!
You see, I know directions
To the left and to the right.
That makes me very bright!

Days of the Week

(sung to "The Eensy-Weensy Spider")

I like when it's Monday,
I help my mother shop.
I like when it's Tuesday,
I watch my bunny hop.
I like when it's Wednesday,
I sit and read a book.
I like when it's Thursday,
I help my father cook.

I like when it's Friday,
I go and climb a tree.
I like when it's Saturday,
I watch my small TV.
I like when it's Sunday,
I play my favorite game.
Which day is my favorite?
I like them all the same!

Months of the Year

(sung to "Here We Go Looby Loo")

CHORUS:
Here we go month to month,
Here we go 'round the year.
Here we go month to month,
All of the months are here!

January is first,
First month of the year,
Then February and March,
Now April is already here!

CHORUS

Next come May and June,
Soon July draws near.
August comes along,
As we go around the year!

CHORUS

September and October,
November now is here,
And last we have December,
The last month of the year!

CHORUS

Four Seasons

(sung to "If you're Happy and You Know It")

If it's spring, it's the time to fly a kite!
If it's spring, it's the time to fly a kite!
If it's spring, it's the season,
You don't need a better reason,
If it's spring, it's the time to fly a kite!

If it's summer, it's the time to take a swim!
If it's summer, it's the time to take a swim!
If it's summer, it's the season,
You don't need a better reason,
If it's summer, it's the time to take a swim!

If it's fall, it's the time to rake the leaves!
If it's fall, it's the time to rake the leaves!
If it's fall, it's the season,
You don't need a better reason,
If it's fall, it's the time to rake the leaves!

If it's winter, it's the time to ride a sled!
If it's winter, it's the time to ride a sled!
If it's winter, it's the season,
You don't need a better reason,
If it's winter, it's the time to ride a sled!

50 Learning Songs Scholastic Professional Books

Telling Time

(sung to "The Farmer in the Dell")

CHORUS:

**It's time to tell the time,
It's time to tell the time,
Check your clock, and check your watch,
It's time to tell the time!**

The big hand's on the 12,
The little hand's on the 3,
It means the time is 3 o'clock,
It's time to tell the time!

CHORUS

The big hand's on the 12,
The little hand's on the 6,
It means the time is 6 o'clock,
It's time to tell the time!

CHORUS

The big hand's on the 12,
The little hand's on the 9,
It means the time is 9 o'clock,
It's time to tell the time!

CHORUS

The big hand's on the 12,
The little hand's on the 12,
It means the time is 12 o'clock,
It's time to tell the time!

CHORUS

Money

(sung to "Miss Lucy Had a Baby")

Miss Lucy had a **penny**,
That means she had a cent.
She kept on saving pennies,
Then to the bank she went.

She traded in her pennies,
And got a **nickel** back.
She kept on saving nickels,
And piled them in a stack.

She traded in her nickels,
And she got back a **dime**.
She saved her dimes and nickels
For a **quarter** over time.

She kept on saving quarters,
And watched her pile increase,
Then traded in her quarters
For a **half-dollar** piece.

Miss Lucy kept on saving,
She saved some more until
She traded her half dollars
For a single **dollar** bill!

Miss Lucy learned a lesson,
A lesson good to know:
If you save up your money,
Then it will surely grow!

Adding

(sung to "The Ants Go Marching One by One")

Today I'm adding 1 + 1,
It's 2, it's 2.
Today I'm adding 1 + 1,
It's 2, it's 2.
Today, I'm adding 1 + 1,
Adding numbers is so much fun,
Today I've learned that
1 + 1 are 2.

Today I'm adding 2 + 2,
It's 4, it's 4.
Today I'm adding 2 + 2,
It's 4, it's 4.
Today I'm adding 2 + 2,
Adding numbers is fun to do,
Today I've learned that
2 + 2 are 4.

Today I'm adding 4 + 4,
It's 8, it's 8.
Today I'm adding 4 + 4,
It's 8, it's 8.
Today I'm adding 4 + 4,
Adding numbers amounts to more,
Today I've learned that
4 + 4 are 8!

Take Away

(sung to "Polly Wolly Doodle All the Day")

5 take away 4 is 1,
1's left when you take away.
5 take away 3 is 2,
2's left when you take away.

CHORUS:

**Take away, take away,
Subtract or take away.
Take the number that is smaller
From the number that is larger.
What's left when you take away?**

8 take away 3 is 5,
5's left when you take away.
8 take away 4 is 4,
4's left when you take away.

50 Learning Songs Scholastic Professional Books

9 take away 6 is 3,
3's left when you take away.
9 take away 7 is 2,
2's left when you take away.

CHORUS

10 take away 2 is 8,
8's left when you take away.
10 take away 4 is 6,
6's left when you take away!

10 take away 1 is 9,
9's left when you take away.
10 take away 10 is 0,
0's left when you take away!

CHORUS

Skip Counting

(sung to "99 Bottles")

Two numbers we skip at a time,
Two numbers we skip,
Yes, we can count a large amount
When two numbers we skip at a time.

2, 4, 6, 8,
10, 12, and more!
14, 16, 18, 20,
Two numbers we skip at a time!

Five numbers we skip at a time,
Five numbers we skip,
Yes, we can count a large amount
When five numbers we skip at a time.

5, 10, 15, 20,
25, 30, and more!
35, 40, 45, 50,
Five numbers we skip at a time!

Ten numbers we skip at a time,
Ten numbers we skip,
Yes, we can count a large amount
When ten numbers we skip at a time.

10, 20, 30, 40,
50, 60, and more!
70, 80, 90, 100,
Ten numbers we skip at a time!

Patterns

(sung to "Alouette")

CHORUS:
Find a pattern, can you find a pattern?
Find a pattern, something that repeats.

1 and 2 and 1 and 2,
1 and 2 and 1 and 2,
1 and 2, 1 and ___ (2), oh!

CHORUS

A and B and C and D,
A and B and C and D,
A and B, C and ___ (D), oh!

CHORUS

Round and round and round and square,
Round and round and round and square,
Round and round, round and ___ (square), oh!

CHORUS

Red and green and green and red,
Red and green and green and red,
Red and green, green and ___ (red), oh!

CHORUS

Pairs

(sung to "This Old Man, He Played One")

What's a pair? One and one!
Using pairs is so much fun!
When you've got a pair,
It means that there are two.
Using pairs is fun to do!

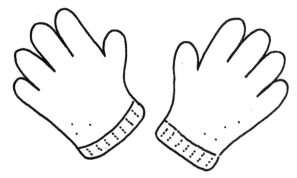

A pair of hands, a pair of feet,
A pair of legs to cross the street!
When you've got a pair,
It means that there are two.
Using pairs is fun to do!

A pair of socks, a pair of shoes,
A pair of gloves for you to choose!
When you've got a pair,
It means that there are two.
Using pairs is fun to do!

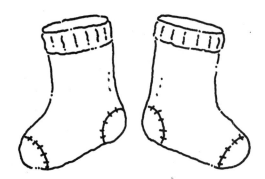

A pair of eyes, a pair of ears,
A pair of friends to play for years!
When you've got a pair,
It means that there are two.
Using pairs is fun to do!

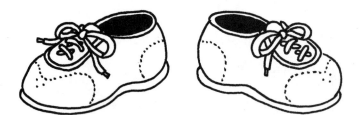

50 Learning Songs Scholastic Professional Books

Fractions

(sung to "When the Saints Go Marching In")

Oh, when a pizza's cut in half,
Oh, when a pizza's cut in half,
There are equal parts for two people,
When a pizza's cut in half.

Oh, when a pizza's cut in thirds,
Oh, when a pizza's cut in thirds,
There are equal parts for three people,
When a pizza's cut in thirds.

Oh, when a pizza's cut in fourths,
Oh, when a pizza's cut in fourths,
There are equal parts for four people,
When a pizza's cut in fourths.

Oh, when a pizza's cut in fifths,
Oh, when a pizza's cut in fifths,
There are equal parts for five people,
When a pizza's cut in fifths.

Weigh and Measure

(sung to "London Bridge Is Falling Down")

CHORUS:

Weigh and measure, oh what fun!
Oh, what fun! Oh, what fun!
Weigh and measure, oh what fun!
Weigh and measure!

Weigh the ounces, weigh the pounds,
Weigh the tons, oh what fun!
Weigh the carats, weigh the grams,
Weigh and measure!

CHORUS

Measure inches, measure feet,
Measure yards, oh how neat!
Measure meters, measure miles,
Weigh and measure!

CHORUS

Measure pints and measure cups,
Measure quarts, add them up.
Measure gallons, measure liters,
Weigh and measure!

CHORUS

Library

(sung to "Pussycat, Pussycat")

Library, library,
What's on the shelf?
All kinds of books
I can read by myself!
Library, library,
What do I see?
Lots of good books
I can check out for free!

Library, library,
What do you hold?
Newspapers, magazines,
Both new and old.
Library, library,
Which should I choose?
I'll pick a good article
And read the news!

Library, library,
What else is there?
Records and videos
Stacked everywhere!
Library, library,
You're what I need,
A place I can visit
To learn and to read!

School

(sung to "Skip to My Lou")

CHORUS:

School, school, let's go to school,
School, school, let's go to school,
School, school, let's go to school,
Let's go to school and learn there!

I love reading, yes I do,
Storybooks are fun, it's true!
Let me read aloud to you,
Let's go to school and learn there!

CHORUS

I love math, it's fun to add,
One, two, three—now that's not bad!
Counting numbers makes me glad,
Let's go to school and learn there!

CHORUS

50 Learning Songs Scholastic Professional Books

I love science, what a treat!
Plants and stars just can't be beat!
Animals are, oh, so neat!
Let's go to school and learn there!

CHORUS

I love writing, it's such fun,
Wrote a story for someone,
Now my poem's almost done,
Let's go to school and learn there!

CHORUS

The Market

(sung to "Take Me Out to the Ball Game")

Take me out to the market,
Take out me to the store,
Show me the fruits and the veggies there,
Show me bread, eggs, and fish everywhere!

Let me shop, shop, shop for some pizza,
Shop, shop, shop for some meat,
For it's fun to go to the market
For food we eat!

Take me out to the market,
Take me out to the store,
Show me the cereals, if you please,
Show me noodles, and show me the cheese!

Let me shop, shop, shop for some ice cream,
Shop, shop, shop for some rice,
For it's fun to be at the market,
A place so nice!

50 Learning Songs Scholastic Professional Books

At the Fire Station

(sung to "Down by the Station")

Down at the station,
At the fire station,
See the fire engines,
Ready for the call.
Holding the hoses,
Holding the ladders,
Holding equipment,
For fires big or small.

Down at the station,
At the fire station,
See the fire fighters,
Ready and alert.
Wearing their fire coats,
Wearing their fire hats,
Wearing their fire boots,
So no one will get hurt.

The United States

(sung to "The Old Gray Mare")

The U.S.A. is made up of 50 states,
Made up of 50 states, made up of 50 states.
The U.S.A. is made up of 50 states
In the United States!

The U.S.A. was born in 1776,
Born in 1776, born in 1776.
The U.S.A. was born in 1776,
That's our United States!

The U.S.A. is home to Americans,
Home to Americans, home to Americans.
The U.S.A. is home to Americans
In the United States!

The U.S.A. is led by the President,
Led by the President, led by the President.
The U.S.A. is led by the President
Of the United States!

The U.S.A. gives freedom to everyone,
Freedom to everyone, freedom to everyone.
The U.S.A. gives freedom to everyone
In the United States!

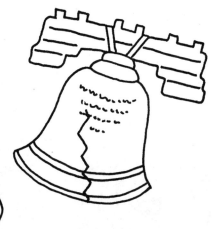

50 Learning Songs Scholastic Professional Books

The President

(sung to "Where Have You Been, Billy Boy")

Tell me, what do you do,
President, President?
Tell me, what do you do
When you lead us?
Once a new law has been made,
I make sure that it's obeyed,
And I help other countries
When they need us!

Tell me, where do you work,
President, President?
Tell me, where do you work
When you lead us?
I'm in Washington, D.C.,
In the White House you see me,
Where I greet lots of visitors
Who meet us!

Our Flag

(sung to "Yankee Doodle Went to Town")

Waving freely is our flag,
And I salute it proudly.
I pledge allegiance to the flag
And say it nice and loudly!

CHORUS:

Proudly waving is the flag,
Symbol of our nation.
See the famous stars and stripes,
Oh, what a fine creation!

50 stars of blue and white,
For 50 states we now have!
13 stripes of red and white,
For colonies we once had!

CHORUS

Hello Around the World

(sung to "This Land Is Your Land")

CHORUS:

**All around the world,
Everywhere you go,
There's a special way
People say hello!
When you are traveling
To different places,
That's another way to say hello!**

If you're in China, you'll hear "NEE-how,"
If you're in Russia, you'll hear "PREE-vee-et,"
If you're in Mexico, you'll hear "OH-lah,"
That's another way to say hello!

CHORUS

If you're in France, you'll hear "bon-JOOR,"
If you're in Hawaii, you'll hear "ah-LOH-ha,"
If you're in Israel, you'll hear "shah-LOM,"
That's another way to say hello!

CHORUS

If you're in Italy, you'll hear "CHOW,"
If you're in Egypt, you'll hear "MAH-hah-bah,"
If you're in Greece, you'll hear "yah-SOO,"
That's another way to say hello!

CHORUS

Russia

China

Hawaii

France

Italy

Egypt

December Holidays

(sung to "Here We Go 'Round the Mulberry Bush")

CHORUS:

Oh, how we love to celebrate,
To celebrate, to celebrate,
Oh, how we love to celebrate
The holidays of December!

Hanukkah is for eight nights.
Light the bright menorah lights!
Potato pancakes! Take big bites!
Hannukah comes in December!

CHORUS

Christmas time is time for glee.
Decorate the Christmas tree!
Look what Santa left for me!
Christmas comes in December!

CHORUS

Kwanzaa lasts for seven days,
Kinara candles proudly blaze!
Feast and laugh and talk and praise!
Kwanzaa comes in December!

CHORUS

50 Learning Songs Scholastic Professional Books

The Pilgrims

(sung to "Oh, Susanna")

Oh, they left their homes in England
And prepared to take a trip.
They climbed aboard the Mayflower,
And sailed upon the ship.

The year was 1620,
On a cold November day,
By the shores of Massachusetts,
They arrived in Plymouth Bay.

CHORUS:

Oh, the Pilgrims!
Seeking to be free!
They came here to America
For opportunity!

The first year was the hardest,
But their neighbors helped them out.
They met Native Americans
With Squanto as their scout.

He helped the Pilgrims plant the crops
Of pumpkins, beans, and corn.
They shared a feast, and that is how
Thanksgiving Day was born!

CHORUS

Say "Please"

(sung to "Three Blind Mice")

Just say please, just say please,
Please pass the bread, please pass the cheese.
If you want someone to help you out,
No need to worry, no need to shout,
The best solution, without a doubt,
Is just say "Please."

Just say please, just say please,
Please hold the door, please get the keys.
If you want someone to help you out,
No need to worry, no need to shout,
The best solution, without a doubt,
Is just say "Please."

Say "Thank You"

(sung to "Sailing, Sailing")

"Thank you, thank you!"
That is the thing to say
When someone tells you something nice
Like "You look great today!"
"Thank you, thank you!"
That is the best reply.
If someone pays a compliment,
Say "thank you"—don't be shy!

"Thank you, thank you!"
That is the thing to say,
If you receive a present,
Offer "thank you" right away!
"Thank you, thank you!"
That is the thing to do.
If you tell people "thank you,"
They will think a lot of you!

"Thank you, thank you!"
That is the thing to say,
When someone holds the door for you
Or asks if you can play.
"Thank you, thank you!"
These are the words so right.
When anyone is kind to you,
Say "thank you"—be polite!

Solving Problems

(sung to "Did You Ever See a Lassie?")

CHORUS:

If you ever have a problem,
A problem, a problem,
If you ever have a problem,
Then let's talk it out!

Let's look at our choices,
And speak in calm voices,
If you ever have a problem,
Then let's talk it out!

CHORUS

Let's all do the right thing,
The kind and polite thing,
If you ever have a problem,
Then let's talk it out!

50 Learning Songs Scholastic Professional Books

Sharing

(sung to "Daisy, Daisy")

Sharing, sharing,
What a nice thing to do.
Share with me and
I'll also share with you.
Let's go to the park on Sunday,
We both will have a fun day!
You share your drum,
I'll share my plum,
Because sharing is fun, it's true!

Sharing, sharing,
Sharing is such a joy.
Sharing cookies,
Sharing a brand-new toy.
No matter the time or weather,
It's great to share together,
You share your cat,
I'll share my bat,
Because sharing is fun, oh boy!

Taking Turns

(sung to "Little Brown Jug")

CHORUS:
A turn for you, a turn for me,
Taking turns is fun, you see!
A turn for me, a turn for you,
Taking turns is fun to do!

Have you seen my new bike?
You can ride it if you like!
You ride first, then I'll go,
Taking turns is great, you know!

CHORUS

I see you have a game.
Gee, I wish I had the same!
Do you mind if I play?
Taking turns is the best way!

CHORUS

When it's time to feed our pet,
Here's a way we won't forget.
First you feed, then I feed,
Taking turns is what we need!

CHORUS

50 Learning Songs Scholastic Professional Books

Listening

(sung to "Frère Jacques")

Are you listening? Are you listening?
Listen well, listen well.
If someone else is speaking,
If someone else is speaking,
Listen well, listen well.

Are you listening? Are you listening?
Now hear this, now hear this.
Be sure to pay attention,
Be sure to pay attention,
Now hear this, now hear this.

Are you listening? Are you listening?
Don't interrupt, don't interrupt.
If someone else is talking,
If someone else is talking,
Don't interrupt, don't interrupt.

Are you listening? Are you listening?
Listen close, listen close.
Think what you are hearing,
Think what you are hearing,
Listen close, listen close.

Friendship

(sung to "Camptown Races")

What's the best thing we can share?
Friendship! Friendship!
How can we both show we care?
Let's be caring friends!
I like you, and you like me,
Friendship! Friendship!
What's the nicest thing to be?
Let's be caring friends!

CHORUS:

Being a friend all day,
Being a friend all night.
Whether times are glad or sad,
Friends can make them right!

I'll help you when you are down,
Friendship! Friendship!
Make you smile if you should frown,
Let's be caring friends!
You help me if things go wrong,
Friendship! Friendship!
Help each other all day long,
Let's be caring friends!

CHORUS

Animal Sounds

(sung to "Baa Baa Black Sheep")

Sheep say "Baa" and cows say "Moo."
Horses "Neigh" and owls say "Hoo."
Ducks say "Quack" and lions "Roar!"
Geese say "Honk" then "Honk" some more.
Pigs say "Oink" and pigeons "Coo."
Hear them at the farm or zoo!

Bees say "Buzz" and crows say "Caw."
Donkeys give a loud "Hee haw!"
Birds say "Chirp" and wolves say "Howl."
Snakes say "Hiss" and bears say "Growl!"
Roosters "Cock-a-doodle-doo."
Hear them at the farm or zoo!

Animal Groups

(sung to "Goodnight, Ladies")

Hello, mammals! Hello, mammals! Hello, mammals!
It's great to have you here!
Merrily you go along! Tiger, bat, dog, and cat!
Horse and sheep and cow and rat!
It's great to have you here!

Hello, insects! Hello, insects! Hello, insects!
It's great to have you here!
Merrily you go along! Beetle, fly, passing by!
Hey, grasshopper hopping high!
It's great to have you here!

Hello, birds! Hello, birds! Hello, birds!
It's great to have you here!
Merrily you go along! Cardinal, wren, owl, and hen!
Turkey trotting in your pen!
It's great to have you here!

Hello, fish! Hello, fish! Hello, fish!
It's great to have you here!
Merrily you go along! Tuna, trout, splash about!
Swordfish with a pointed snout!
It's great to have you here!

Hello, reptiles! Hello, reptiles! Hello, reptiles!
It's great to have you here!
Merrily you go along! Turtle, snake, by the lake!
Crocodile, for goodness sake!
It's great to have you here!

Eggs

(sung to "It Ain't Gonna' Rain No More")

CHORUS:

Who's gonna lay an egg, an egg?
Who's gonna lay an egg?
Which baby animals now will hatch?
Who's gonna lay an egg, an egg?

Hens lay eggs, ducks lay eggs,
Geese lay eggs as well.
Baby birds hatch from eggs,
Who's gonna lay an egg, an egg?

CHORUS

Fish lay eggs, frogs lay eggs,
Snakes lay eggs as well.
Baby turtles hatch from eggs.
Who's gonna lay an egg, an egg?

CHORUS

Life of a Frog

(sung to "Mary Had a Little Lamb")

Frog just laid a little egg,
Little egg, little egg.
Frog just laid a little egg,
And now a tadpole's hatched.

Tadpole looks just like a fish,
Like a fish, like a fish.
Tadpole looks just like a fish,
It swims and starts to grow.

Tadpole now is growing legs,
Growing legs, growing legs.
Tadpole now is growing legs,
Its body's getting big.

Tadpole's grown into a frog,
To a frog, to a frog.
Tadpole's grown into a frog,
Now watch it leap and hop!

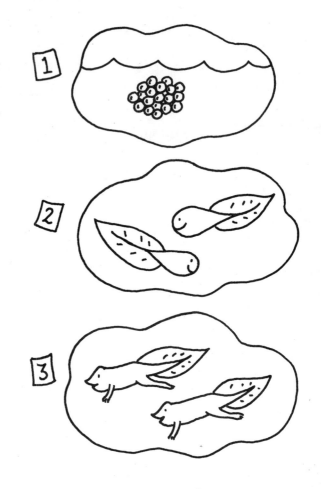

Bugs

(sung to "Home on the Range")

Oh, give me a home
Where the bugs like to roam,
Where they crawl or they swim or they fly!
Way up in the trees,
Sailing high in the breeze,
Or afloat in a stream passing by.

CHORUS:

Bugs, bugs all around,
In the air, in the trees, on the ground!
On flowers and plants,
There's a very good chance
That a lot of small bugs can be found!

I see bumblebees,
Also beetles and fleas,
There are flies and mosquitoes and ants.
The crickets are near,
Many June bugs are here,
And the moths are all munching on plants!

CHORUS

Dressing for Weather

(sung to "Hush, Little Baby, Don't Say a Word")

What should you wear when you go outside?
Look at the weather and then decide.

If it's a hot and sunny day,
A short-sleeved shirt and shorts are okay.

But if the wind is chilly and bold,
Wear pants and a sweater, don't catch cold!

If you should see a rainy sky,
A raincoat and boots will keep you dry.

And if there's snow that falls in a storm,
A coat, scarf, and gloves will keep you warm.

What should you wear when you go outside?
Look at the weather and then decide.

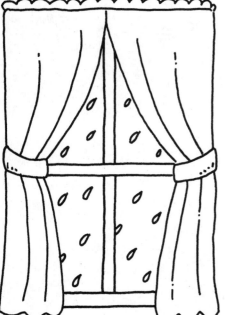

Five Senses

(sung to "The Wheels on the Bus")

The eyes that I have I use to see,
Use to see, use to see.
The eyes that I have I use to see,
See everything!

The ears that I have I use to hear,
Use to hear, use to hear.
The ears that I have I use to hear,
Hear everything!

The nose that I have I use to smell,
Use to smell, use to smell.
The nose that I have I use to smell,
Smell everything!

The hands that I have I use to touch,
Use to touch, use to touch.
The hands that I have I use to touch,
Touch everything!

The tongue that I have I use to taste,
Use to taste, use to taste.
The tongue that I have I use to taste,
Taste everything!

My Body

(sung to "There's a Hole in the Bucket")

There are legs on my body
For walking and running.
There are legs on my body
For walking all day.

There are knees on my body
For bending, for bending.
There are knees on my body
For bending my legs.

There are arms on my body
For throwing and swinging.
There are arms on my body
For throwing a ball.

There are lungs in my body
For breathing, for breathing.
There are lungs in my body
For breathing the air.

There's a heart in my body
For pumping, for pumping.
There's a heart in my body
For pumping my blood.

There's a brain in my body
For thinking, for thinking.
There's a brain in my body
For thinking my thoughts.

All the parts of my body
Are working together.
All the parts of my body
Are working for me!

Trees

(sung to "For He's a Jolly Good Fellow")

CHORUS:

Trees are very good plants,
Trees are very good plants,
Trees are very good plants,
For all the things they do!

They grow the fruit we eat,
Like pears and plums so sweet!

CHORUS

They give us lots of shade
On summer days we play!

CHORUS

They make a cozy home
For birds and bugs to roam.

CHORUS

50 Learning Songs Scholastic Professional Books

They give us lots of wood
For making paper goods.

CHORUS

They help to clean the air
We breathe in everywhere!

CHORUS

They're beautiful to see,
There's nothing like a tree!

CHORUS

Planting a Garden

(sung to "I've Been Working on the Railroad")

I've been working in my garden,
Planting pretty flowers.
I've been working in my garden,
Digging in the soil for hours.
Can you see a daisy blooming?
Look! There's a tulip and a rose!
I've been working in my garden,
Where each pretty flower grows!

I've been working in my garden,
Planting vegetables seeds.
I've been working in my garden,
Giving water each plant needs.
Can you see the beets and carrots?
Look! There's a row of lima beans!
I've been working in my garden,
Growing lots of healthy greens!

Spinach   Carrots   Beets   Lima Beans

Sun and Moon

(sung to "Sing a Song of Sixpence")

Sing a song of sunlight,
All through the day.
Warming up the earth
With each sunny ray.
Rising in the east and
Setting in the west,
Giving us the heat we need,
Oh, sun, you are the best!

Sing a song of moonlight,
All through the night,
Shining in the darkness,
So round and white.
With the stars about you,
See how you glow.
Giving us the light we need,
Oh, moon, we love you so!

Book Links

Reading & Writing

Alphabet Riddles by Susan Joyce (Peel Productions, 1998).

Anna Banana: 101 Jump-Rope Rhymes by J. Cole (Morrow/Avon, 1989).

Chicka Chicka Boom! Boom! By Bill Martin, Jr. and John Archambault (Simon & Schuster, 1989).

I Read Signs by Tana Hoban (William Morrow, 1987).

Merry-Go-Round: A Book About Nouns by Ruth Heller (Penguin Putnam, 1998).

Mine, All Mine: A Book About Pronouns by Ruth Heller (Penguin Putnam, 1997).

Miss Mary Mack and Other Children's Street Rhymes by J. Cole & S Calmenson (Morrow/Avon, 1990).

On Market Street by Arnold Lobel (Greenwillow, 1981).

The Z Was Zapped: A Play in Twenty-Six Acts (Houghton Mifflin, 1987).

Primary Concepts

Chicken Soup With Rice by Maurice Sendak (Harper & Row, 1962).

January Brings the Snow: A Book of Months by Jenni Oliver (Dial, 1986).

Jump for Joy: A Book of Months by Megan Halsey (Bradbury Press, 1994).

My Steps by Sally Derby (Lee & Low Books, 1999).

One Monday Morning by Uri Shulevitz (Scribner, 1967).

The Seasons of Arnold's Apple Tree by Gail Gibbons (Harcourt Children's Books, 1988).

Today Is Monday by Eric Carle (Penguin Putnam, 1997).

Wake Me in Spring by James Preller (Scholastic, 1994).

Mathematics

Billy's Button by William Accorsi (Greenwillow, 1992).

A Chair for My Mother by Vera B. Williams (Greenwillow, 1982).

Domino Addition by Lynette Long, Ph.D. (Charlesbridge, 1996).

The Greedy Triangle by Marilyn Burns (Scholastic, 1994).

Inch by Inch by Leo Leonni (Astor-Honor Publishing, 1960).

Keeping Time by Franklyn M. Branley (Houghton Mifflin, 1993).

Measuring Penny by Loreen Leedy (Henry Holt & Company, 1997).

A Pig Is Big by Douglas Florian (Greenwillow, 2000).

Time to… by Bruce McMillan (Lothrop, Lee & Shephard, 1989).

The Village of Round and Square Houses by Ann Grifalconi (Little Brown & Co., 1986).

Social Studies

Hanukkah by Roni Schotter (Little Brown & Co., 1990).

Imani's Gift at Kwanza by Denise Burden-Patman (Simon & Schuster, 1992).

In 1492 by Jean Marzollo (Scholastic, 1991).

This Land Is Your Land by Woody Guthrie (Little, Brown, 1998).

Let's Visit the Fire Station by Marianne Johnston (Rosen Publishing Group, 2000).

Samuel Eaton's Day: A Day in the Life of a Pilgrim Boy by Kate Waters (Scholastic, 1993).

We the People: Poems by Bobbie Katz (Greenwillow, 2000).

The Wild Reindeer Christmas by Jan Brett (The Putnam Grosset Group, 1990).

Social Skills

Amos & Boris by William Steig (Farrar, Straus & Giroux, 1971).

Best Friends by Miriam Cohen (Simon & Schuster, 1973).

Bright Eyes, Brown Skin by Cheryl Hudson and Bernette Ford (Scholastic, 1990).

Crow Boy by Tara Yashima (Viking, 1995).

It's a Spoon, Not a Shovel by Caralyn Buehner (Dial Books, 1995).

Manners by Aliki (Greenwillow Books, 1990).

Matthew and Tilly by Rebecca C. Jones (Puffin Books, 1995).

Sing Sophie! by Dale Ann Dodds (Candlewick Press, 1997).

Together by George Ella Lyon (Orchard Books, 1989).

Science

Animals and Where They Live by John Feltwell (Dorling Kindersley Ltd., 1992).

Backyard Bugs by Robin Kittrell Laughlin (Chronicle Books, 1996).

Caps, Hats, Socks, and Mittens by Louise Borden (Scholastic, 1989).

Frogs by Gail Gibbons (Holiday House, 1993).

Grandfather Twilight by Barbara Berger (Philomel Books, 1984).

How to hide a Crocodile & Other Reptiles by Ruth Heller (Penguin Putnam, 1994).

The Lorax by Dr. Seuss (Random House, 1971).

My Five Senses by Aliki (Crowell, 1989).

Rechenka's Eggs by Patricia Polacco (Philomel, 1988).

Ruth Heller's How to Hide a Polar Bear & Other Mammals (Turtleback Books, 1994).

The Tiny Seed by Eric Carle (Picture Book Studio, 1987).